THE REASONS FOR SEASONS

New and Updated

HOLIDAY HOUSE
NEW YORK

BY GAIL GIBBONS

To Ken and Maude Ames

Special thanks to Professor Edward Foley,
teacher of astronomy, St. Michael's College,
Colchester, Vermont, and Chris Vaccaro,
National Oceanic and Atmospheric Administration.

Copyright © 1995, 2019 by Gail Gibbons
All Rights Reserved
HOLIDAY HOUSE is registered in the U.S. Patent and Trademark Office.
Printed and bound in May 2021 at Toppan Leefung, DongGuan City, China.
www.holidayhouse.com
Second Edition, New and Updated
5 7 9 10 8 6 4

The Library of Congress has cataloged the prior edition as follows:
Gibbons, Gail.
The reasons for seasons / by Gail Gibbons.—1st ed.
    p.   cm.
ISBN 0-06-021603-4.–ISBN 0-06-021604-2 (lib. bdg.)
1. Seasons—Juvenile literature. [1. Seasons.]   I. Title.
QL696.C42G53 1995   90-30525
598'.33–dc20   CIP   AC

Second Edition, New and Updated
ISBN 978-0-8234-4273-7 (hardcover)
ISBN 978-0-8234-4272-0 (paperback)

Spring. Summer. Autumn. Winter. These are the four seasons of the year.

SUN

EARTH

The sun warms the surface of Earth, the planet we live on. The tilt of Earth in relation to the sun changes throughout the year. This is what makes the seasons.

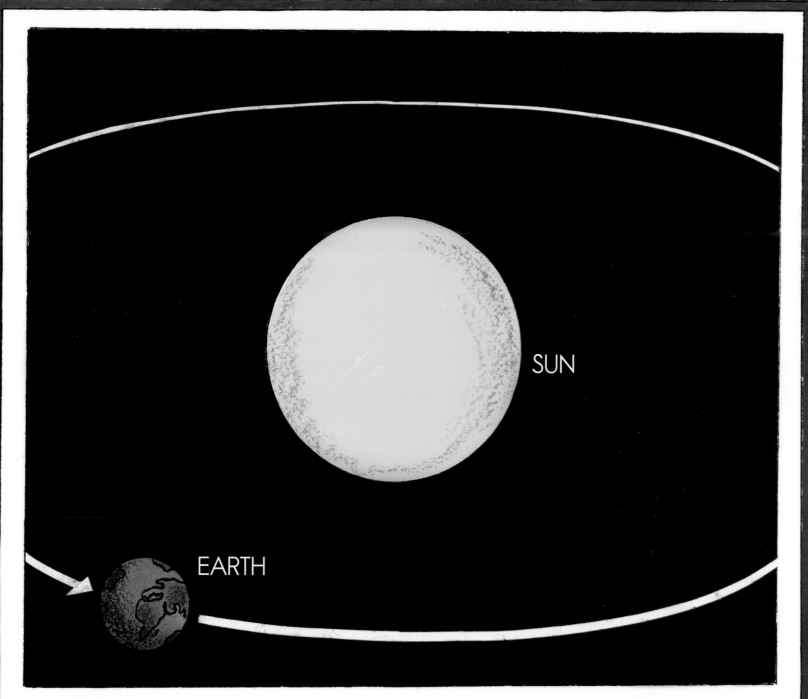

Each season lasts about three months. Four seasons make a year. That's how long it takes for Earth to revolve, or make one trip, around the sun. As Earth circles the sun, different parts of Earth are closer to the sun than others. This affects the amount of light and heat they receive.

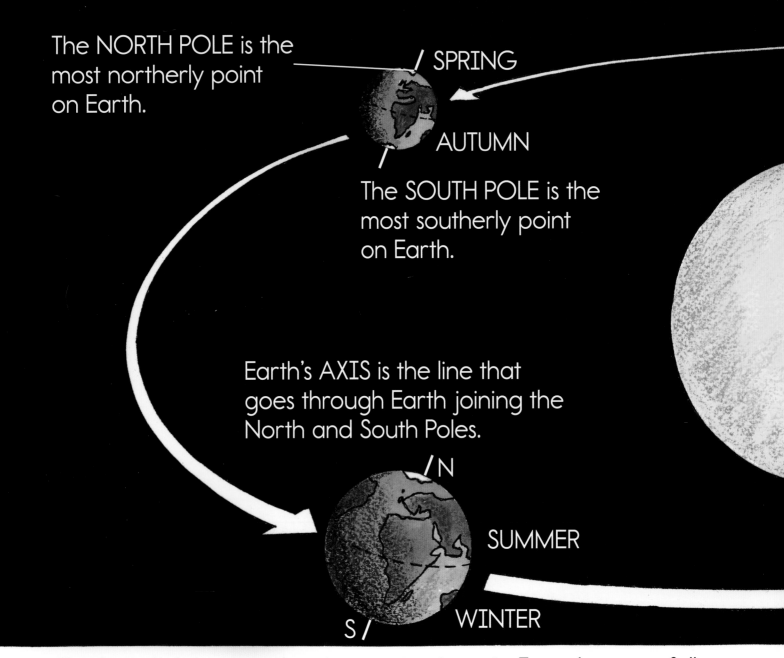

The NORTH POLE is the most northerly point on Earth.

SPRING

AUTUMN

The SOUTH POLE is the most southerly point on Earth.

Earth's AXIS is the line that goes through Earth joining the North and South Poles.

N

SUMMER

WINTER

S

Earth is slightly tipped as it turns on its axis. It makes one full rotation on its axis every 24 hours as it moves along its path around the sun. When the North Pole is tipped toward the sun and the South Pole is tipped away, it is summer in the Northern Hemisphere and winter in the Southern Hemisphere.

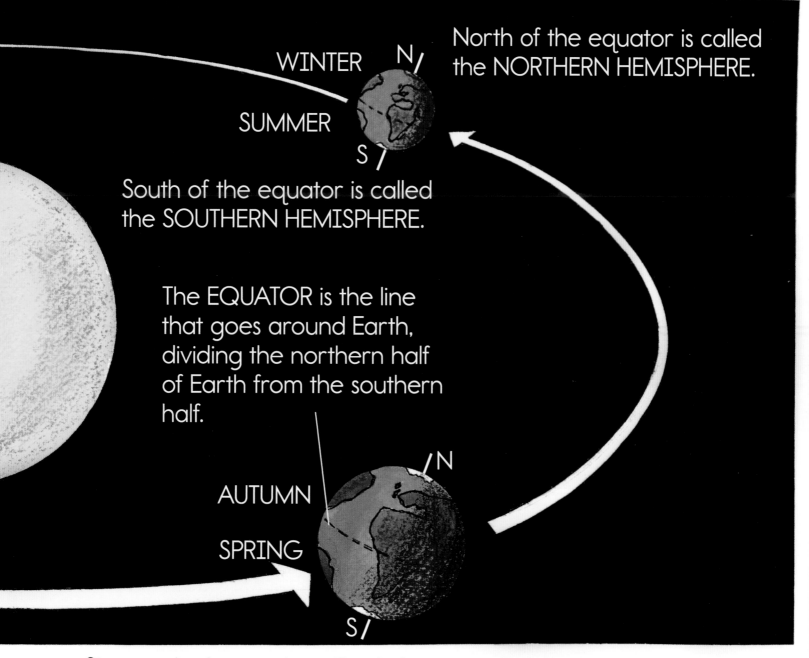

WINTER

N

North of the equator is called the NORTHERN HEMISPHERE.

SUMMER

S

South of the equator is called the SOUTHERN HEMISPHERE.

The EQUATOR is the line that goes around Earth, dividing the northern half of Earth from the southern half.

N

AUTUMN

SPRING

S

Six months later, when Earth has traveled to the other side of the sun and the North Pole is tipped away, it is winter in the Northern Hemisphere and summer in the Southern Hemisphere. The seasons of one hemisphere are always opposite of those in the other hemisphere.

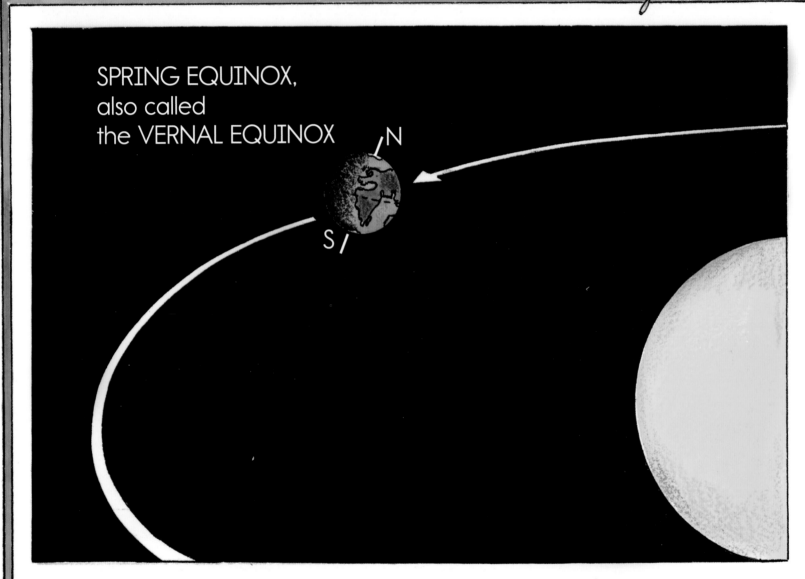

SPRING EQUINOX,
also called
the VERNAL EQUINOX

N

S

In the Northern Hemisphere spring begins about March 21. This is the season when more sunshine causes cooler air to be replaced by warmer air. In the Southern Hemisphere autumn is beginning.

The first day of spring is called the spring equinox. When spring begins in the Northern Hemisphere, Earth has moved along its path so that the sun is directly opposite the equator. On this day, daylight and darkness are the same length of time over the entire Earth. In ancient times some people celebrated this day because it was the beginning of the growing season.

MIGRATION

Spring is the season when some birds that have been away for the winter return again. This is called migration. Some whales migrate, too. Some animals that slept all winter wake up and look for food. Spring winds are good for kite flying.

It is the season when everything seems to come alive again. Trees grow new leaves and flowers bloom. Some crops are planted.

Slowly the days in the Northern Hemisphere become longer because that part of Earth is tilted more toward the sun. We see the sun higher in the sky. More direct sunlight reaches the ground for longer periods of time.

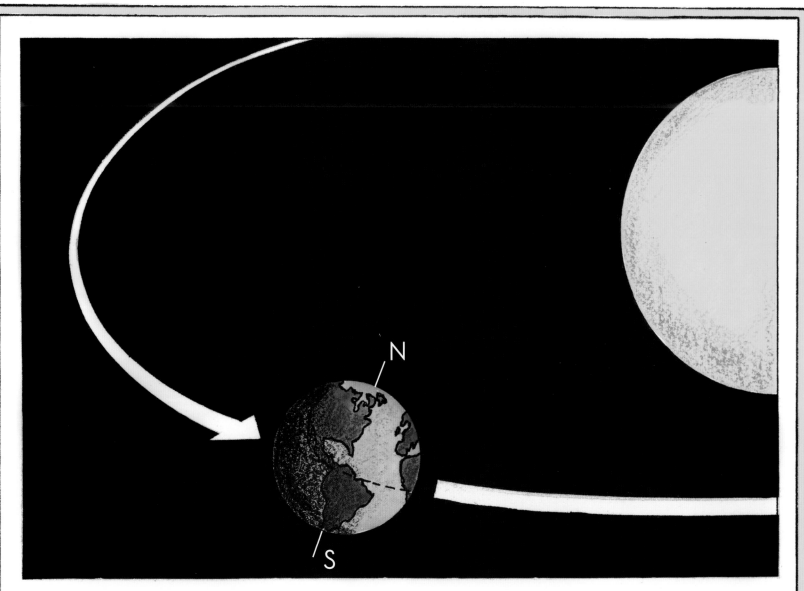

Summer begins in the Northern Hemisphere about June 21. The Northern Hemisphere is tilted more toward the sun than at any other time of the year. It is the warmest season. In the Southern Hemisphere winter is beginning.

N

SUMMER
SOLSTICE

S

The first day of summer is called the summer solstice. It is the longest day of the year. On this day we see the midday sun at its highest point in the sky.

The hottest days of the summer take place after the summer solstice because Earth keeps absorbing more heat. Flowers and plants grow under the warm sun. Many animals are busy raising new families.

In the summertime people have fun outdoors. They can go to a beach, swim in a lake, or read under the shade of a big tree full of large green leaves.

During the summer daylight is long. We see the sun high in the sky. It might still be daylight at bedtime. The nights are shorter.

AUTUMN

Autumn begins about September 21 in the Northern Hemisphere. It is the season when the air starts to get cooler. The leaves of some trees turn to beautiful colors and fall to the ground, which is why some people call this season "fall." In the Southern Hemisphere spring is beginning.

AUTUMNAL EQUINOX

N

S

The first day of autumn is called the autumnal equinox. When autumn begins in the Northern Hemisphere, Earth has moved along its path so that the sun is directly opposite the equator again. On this day, daylight and darkness are about the same length of time over the entire Earth. Since ancient days some people have celebrated this time of year because of the autumn harvest.

Some birds migrate to warmer climates. Animals prepare themselves for the long cold season to come. Children go back to school in many places.

It is harvest season. Farmers gather their crops. There are country fairs, too.

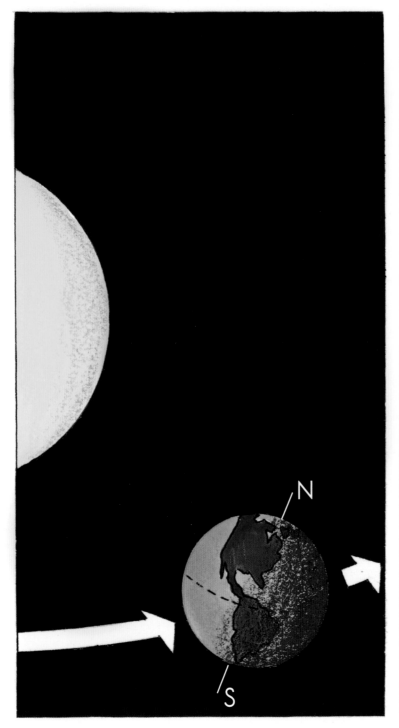

The air becomes cooler because the Northern Hemisphere is tilted farther away from the sun. The days grow shorter and the nights become longer. We see the sun lower in the autumn sky.

In the Northern Hemisphere winter begins about December 21. This is the time of year the Northern Hemisphere is tilted farthest from the sun. It is the coldest season of the year. In the Southern Hemisphere summer is beginning.

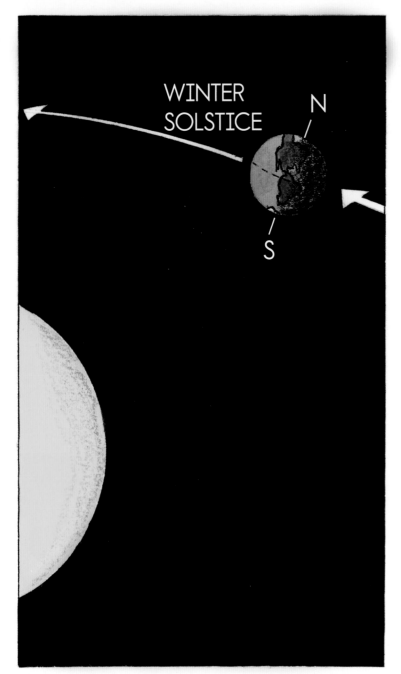

The first day of winter is the shortest day of the year. This is called the winter solstice. On this day we see the midday sun at its lowest point in the sky. In early times the first day of winter was celebrated as a festival to honor light, to keep away darkness, and to hope for the sun's return.

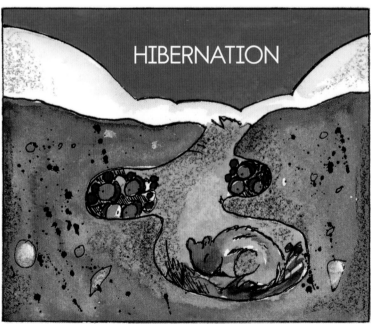
HIBERNATION

The coldest days of the winter come after the winter solstice because Earth keeps losing the heat it gained in the summer. Leaves are gone from most trees. There aren't as many birds. Some animals sleep all winter. This is called hibernation. Often it is very cold.

It may be time for ice skating, skiing, and making snowmen. Some people wear winter coats, jackets, mittens, and hats. Sometimes it is nice to stay indoors.

During winter, daylight is short and the nights are long. We see the sun low in the sky. Sometimes it is dark even before dinner.

Areas near the equator have little temperature change during the year. These places are hardly affected by the tilt of Earth. Instead the seasons are marked by alternating rainy and dry periods, two rainy and two dry seasons each year. Each day at the equator daylight and darkness are almost always equal.

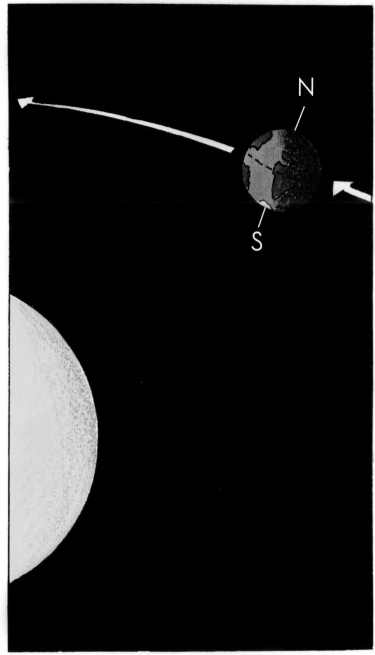

At the North Pole and the South Pole it is always cold. When a pole is tilted far away from the sun it is winter. During parts of the winter, the sun never appears over the horizon. It is always dark. When a pole is tilted closer to the sun it is summer. At times it is always light.

Spring. Summer.

Autumn. Winter. Year after year the seasons repeat themselves.

Seasons...

- In ancient times, some people made stone formations. The stones cast shadows, helping them know the seasons at the time.

- The Egyptians observed three seasons by watching the Nile River. These three were the flooding season, the growing season, and the harvest season.

- The gravitational force of the sun keeps Earth in orbit to create our four seasons.

- Earth is about 93 million miles (150 million km) away from the sun. This creates the perfect orbit position to create the right temperatures for the four seasons.

- The sun is about 110 times the diameter of Earth and more than 300,000 times heavier than Earth.

- The sun is made up of gases that create intense heat. Earth is just the right distance for a livable environment.

- The Parker Solar Probe was recently launched to make a close approach to learn about the sun's energy and its secrets.

- In India, people welcome spring with a festival called Holi, where they sing, dance, and throw colored powder at one another in the streets. The cherry blossom festival, or Hanami, in Japan is a tradition where friends and families celebrate spring by having picnics under the cherry blossoms.

- In the U.S. and Canada, crowds gather on February 2 to watch a groundhog emerge from his burrow. Legend has it that if he sees his shadow, there will be six more weeks of winter, but if he doesn't, there will be an early spring.